How to play
The Pocket
Harmonica

By Peter Pickow & Jason A. Shulman.

D1399482

How to play
The Pocket
Harmonica

By Peter Pickow & Jason A. Shulman.

Cover design by Mike Bell
Cover photography by Peter Wood
Cover diagram by Alison Fenton
Book design by Nina Clayton
Illustrations by Nancy Stevenson
Edited by Louise Moed

Exclusive Distributors:
Music Sales Corporation
257 Park Avenue South, New York, NY 10010 USA
Music Sales Limited
8/9 Frith Street, London W1V 5TZ England
Music Sales Pty. Limited
120 Rothschild Street, Rosebery, Sydney NSW 2018 Australia

Copyright © 1983 by Amsco Publications,
A Division of Music Sales Corporation, New York

All rights reserved. No part of this book may be
reproduced in any form or by any electronic or mechanical means
including information storage and retrieval systems,
without permission in writing from the publisher.

Order No. AM 34521
US ISBN 0.8256.2287.5
UK ISBN 0.7119.0414.6

Printed in the United States of America by
Vicks Lithograph and Printing Corporation

Amsco Publications
New York/London/Sydney

Photo Credits:

19, 57: David Gahr
15: Amy O'Neal
35: Bob Leafe/Star File
42: D. Shigley
46, 53: Chuck Pulin/Star File
47: David Frazer
50: R.L. Boshuizen
55: David Seelig/Star File

from Jason—

To R. Shatkin, secret Brooklyn harp master, who said: "Keep playing until that harp becomes as heavy and big as a boxcar in your hands." And to Ariana Elizabeth, for loving her daddy's harmonica playing.

from Peter—

To my father, George Pickow, who—once upon a time— seemed to me the best harmonica player in the world.

CONTENTS

A LITTLE HARMONICA HISTORY

Harmonicas are everywhere. They show up in movies about World War II ("Hey kid," says the tough Sergeant from Brooklyn, "I don't know if we're gonna get out of this alive. Play me a little tune on your harmonica. . . ."), in movies about the American Civil War ("Hey Private," says the Rebel Captain, "I'm wounded real bad. Play 'Dixie' for me to die by. . . ."), in movies about the Depression ("Hey kid," says one of the tramps gathered around the campfire. . . .), and so on. You'll find harmonicas in car factories, on chain gangs, and in the pockets of singing cowboys.

In the world of blues, pop, jazz, and rock, you will hear harmonica being played by Little Walter, Sonny Boy Williamson, Bob Dylan, Stevie Wonder, Toots Thielemans, Bruce Springsteen, and Magic Dick. You can play any kind of music on harmonica, from classical quartets to country cattle-calls; from sentimental songs around the campfire to rock-and-roll wails to a lonely blues at midnight. The harmonica is at once the easiest and the most demanding of instruments. It is the most vocal and the lightest to carry. By choosing to learn to play harp (as most professional harmonica players fondly call their instrument), you are joining a long line of players who have poured out their hearts through a little piece of tin.

Although the ancient Chinese had a type of harmonica with wooden reeds, and Mozart wrote pieces for a glass harmonica (a completely different instrument consisting of a series of tuned glasses, popular during the 1700s), the diatonic harmonica as we know it today was created in Germany in the early part of the nineteenth century. It was carried to the United States and Great Britain by the waves of immigrants leaving Germany, and by the mid-nineteenth century was played throughout the world.

The chromatic harmonica was invented in 1918. Because it contains all twelve tones of the chromatic scale, it allows you to play much more complicated music, such as jazz and classical pieces. It is also much more complicated to play. It is the simple, diatonic harmonica—

which most people play—that really captured the heart and soul of the world. Over the years, in the hands of the millions of players who have played and loved it, this unassuming, basically chordal instrument has evolved into a singing, shouting, crooning, growling, coaxing, wailing voice with the force of a brass band and the subtlety of a violin.

PICKING YOUR FIRST HARMONICA

Chances are nine out of ten that your first harmonica will be made by the Hohner company. Hohner has been the major manufacturer of harmonicas around the world for about 100 years. Despite an occasional lapse in quality control, they still make the best harp around.

Since this book deals primarily with folk, blues, and rock, you will need a *diatonic* harmonica. This is the most common, simplest, and least expensive type there is. This is not to say that it is limited: almost every professional blues, country, and rock player plays diatonic harp, and the music that you can coax out of one can be truly awe-inspiring.

Hohner makes many models of diatonic harmonica. We recommend choosing among these five: **Marine Band, Golden Melody, Blues Harp, Special Twenty,** and **Old Standby.** They each have the same arrangement of notes and the same basic reed plate (the part that actually produces the sound). The differences lie in the body construction: The Marine Band, Old Standby, and Blues Harp all have wooden bodies; the Golden Melody and Special Twenty have plastic bodies. Because of the slightly different acoustic properties of these materials and the way in which they are assembled each of these styles sounds just a little bit different. Also important is that each one will feel just a little different to your mouth and hands. You can make beautiful music on any of them and the one you choose should be the one that sounds and feels best to you.

In the comparison chart below, all models mentioned have nickel-plated covers. You should try to make a decision with the help of this chart before you go to the music store, as most states have health laws that forbid trying a harmonica before you buy it.

Model (List Price)	Body Material	Reed Plate	Fits in Holder	Comments
Marine Band	wood	brass	yes	the bluesman's standard ax— has a long and noble history
Old Standby	wood	brass	yes	Charlie McCoy swears by its light, flexible tone—good for country playing
Golden Melody	plastic	brass	· no	a newcomer— good, airtight seal
Blues Harp	wood	brass reeds set high	yes	a good beginner's harp—reeds have a tendency to wear out quickly
Special Twenty	plastic	brass	yes	our favorite— sweet tone, air-tight, and rugged body

While you are learning to play, it will not matter what key harmonica you have. Whether it is a C, G, B-flat, or any other key, the setup and sequence of notes will be the same. In the beginning you will probably find the lower keys easier to play. Throughout this book, when it is necessary to refer to notes, keys, or chords, we will discuss them in terms of the C harp for convenience. Eventually you will want to own harmonicas in several keys so that you can jam with other musicians in a variety of situations.

GETTING TO KNOW YOUR HARMONICA

Breaking In Your Harmonica

There is an old tradition which holds that the first thing you should do to a new harmonica is to dunk it in a glass of liquid for ten or twenty minutes. The recommended liquid varies from plain water to draft beer to whiskey to vodka. As much as it seems to be, this is not merely an old harpdog's tale: The liquid swells the wooden body of the harp, making for a more airtight seal between reed plate and body. This does actually work: It can increase the volume of the harp by as much as 100 percent. In the long run, however, it actually shortens the life expectency of the instrument by 100 percent and can turn it into a lethal weapon (at least as far as your tongue and lips are concerned): The wood eventually shrinks back to less than its original size, creating a small gap between body and reed plate that is just big enough to catch some important piece of flesh (ouch!). Our recommendation is that you take the time to break in your harmonica correctly. It will take a little longer than the baptism in beer but your harp will end up sounding better and lasting longer, and you won't be needing stitches in your lips.

For the first few days, blow *gently*. You will find that some of the high notes will not sound too good. Avoid the temptation of blowing as hard as you can, but instead gradually increase the amount of air pressure. After a few hours of playing, all the notes should sound just fine.

The Care and Feeding of Your Harmonica

Taking care of a harmonica is relatively simple (which probably explains why people seldom do it).

Whenever you are not playing it, keep the harmonica in its case. This is especially true if you are carrying it around in your pocket. Dust is one of the great enemies of harmonicas and yours will sound good a lot longer if you keep it clean.

Never play your harmonica directly after eating without first rinsing out your mouth; otherwise you will surely ruin your instrument (to say nothing of the risk of choking when you play a long hard draw note). We leave it to you as to what you rinse out your mouth with.

After you are through playing, slap the harmonica gently against the palm of your hand. The accepted wisdom is to tap the mouthpiece side since the reeds converge toward the reed plate at that end. Our advice is to tap it easily on both sides—if something is stuck in there, you will have a better chance of dislodging it. If something is firmly stuck inside, don't be afraid to give the harp a solid shot against your palm: You cannot really hurt it this way.

Other than these main points, you need do nothing special. The harmonica is a simple instrument and requires little; only that you love it, play it, and get as good as you can on it.

First Steps

Before you play a note, let's examine just how your harmonica works. You can see that it has got ten holes, numbered 1 through 10. Each one of these holes produces two different pitches: one by *blowing* (exhaling) and one by *drawing* (inhaling). So, with only ten holes, you can get twenty notes covering a range of three octaves.

Let's look at the bottom octave first. Hold your harp in your left hand, between thumb and forefinger, with the numbers facing up.

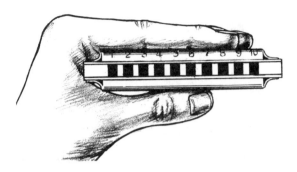

Now, with your teeth slightly parted, mouth and jaw relaxed, lips moist, cover holes 1, 2, and 3, and gently exhale. Even though we call it blowing into the harp, you should think of it more as breathing into it. When you breathe, the air comes from way down inside you, from the diaphragm. Try to imagine the way you breathe just before you fall asleep—that's breathing from the diaphragm. We will talk more about breath control as we go along because it is probably the most important aspect of playing the harmonica.

Keep all this in mind as you draw in on holes 123. In the beginning you will probably find that you actually have to concentrate on staying relaxed. Let your lips curl out naturally. Don't worry if you resemble a trout—that means you are doing something right. If the notes sound slightly fuzzy or distorted, it is probably because your lips are not forming an effective seal and some air is escaping over the top or underneath. Adjust the harp until you get a good seal without tensing up; tension will only make matters worse.

As you breathe in and out on 123, keep your tongue on the bottom of your mouth. You can see that moving it around changes the tone of the notes you are playing. We will bring the tongue into play later when we talk about *tonguing, bending* notes, and other special effects; but for now we want a pure, consistent tone. Pretend that it is time for your annual checkup and say "ah."

Frank Floyd breaking in his harmonica

16

Chords

So far we have played two chords. No matter what key harp you have, these chords are I (blow) and V (draw). (If you have a C harp, the I chord is C and the V chord is G.) These are the two most important chords in any song; in fact, in many songs they are the only chords. As an example, think (or better yet, get someone to sing) the melody to "Frère Jacques" while you back it up with I and V chords. The numbers 123 indicate blow notes; the numbers ⟨123⟩ indicate draw notes.

123	⟨123⟩	123		123	⟨123⟩	123
Frè	- re	Jacques,		frè	- re	Jacques,
123	⟨123⟩	123		123	⟨123⟩	123
Dor	- mez -	vous?		Dor	- mez -	vous?
123	⟨123⟩	123	⟨123⟩	123		
Son	- nez	les	ma -	tines,		
123	⟨123⟩	123	⟨123⟩	123		
Son	- nez	les	ma -	tines:		
123	⟨123⟩	123	123	⟨123⟩	123	
Ding,	dong,	ding;	ding,	dong,	ding.	

Now this may not sound like much, but it's a start.

Tonguing

Before we start to add melodies onto our I and V chords, let's talk about *tonguing*. To tongue a note simply means to whisper the syllable "too" as you breathe into your harp. Touch the tip of your tongue to the roof of your mouth just behind your front teeth. Drop your tongue back to the floor of your mouth and exhale simultaneously into 123—that's tonguing. A lot easier to do than to explain, eh? Tongue a few chords in a row. Then try tonguing the V (draw) chord.

Play the chords to "Frère Jacques" again and tongue each syllable of the words:

tongue:

too	too	too	too	too	too	too	too
123	⟨123⟩	123	123	123	⟨123⟩	123	123
Frè - re		Jac - ques,		frè - re		Jac -	ques, *etc.*

THE BASICS OF PLAYING

Chord Melody

It's time to start playing something that sounds more like music. By playing 123 so much, you should now have a pretty good feel for how to keep your mouth fixed to play three holes at a time. As we start to move up and down the instrument, remember to keep your upper and lower lips relaxed. Keep just a little tension in the sides of your mouth where it touches the harp (not in the cheeks) to maintain the proper size opening.

The basic idea of the chord-melody style is to play three-note or two-note chords with the melody note on top. Here's "Frère Jacques" in chord-melody style:

```
234   (234)    345   234   234   (234)    345   234
Frè -  re      Jac - ques, frè -  re      Jac - ques,
345   (345)          456   345   (345)          456
Dor - mez  -         vous? Dor - mez  -         vous?
456   (456) 456  (345) 345   234
Son -  nez les   ma -  ti  -  nes,
456   (456) 456  (345) 345   234
Son -  nez les   ma -  ti  -  nes:
234   (12)     234   234   (12)     234
Ding,  dong,   ding; ding, dong,   ding.
```

Listen to your playing carefully to make sure that you are playing all the notes of each chord.

Before we get down to some more tunes, practice these two chord scales. If you learn them well, they will take you a long way toward being able to figure out songs on your own.

Chord scale 1

```
234 (234) 345 (345) 456 (456)(567) 567
Do   re   mi   fa   so   la   ti   do
```

Chord scale 2

34 (34) 45 (45) 56 (56)(67) 67
Do re mi fa so la ti do

Chord-Melody Tunes

The tunes that follow are all written in the three-note chord style but you can play them with two-note harmony by using only the two higher numbers. In some places two-note chords are indicated (i.e., the "old" in "My Old Kentucky Home"). This is because the actual chord for these notes is neither I nor V but IV (F in the key of C). If you are playing solo, you can add the bottom note if you like the sound, but if someone is backing you up and playing the IV chord, it will clash. We will talk more about the IV chord later.

Oh, My Darling Clementine
234 234 234 123   345 345 345 234
In   a   cav - ern,   in   a   can - yon,
234 345 456 456 (345) 345 (234)
Ex - ca - va - ting for   a   mine,
(234)   345 (345)(345)(345) 345 (234) 345 234
Lived   a   miner,   a   forty - niner,
234 345 (234) (12) (123)(234) 234
And his   daughter ,   Clementine.

My Old Kentucky Home
234 (234) 345 345   234
Oh the sun shines bright
(234) 345 (45) 45 (45)(56)   456
On my old Kentucky home,
(45) 345 (234) 234   234 (123)   234 (234)
'Tis summer, the   folks there are gay;
345 345 345   234
The corntop's ripe
(234) 345 (45) 45   (45)(56)   456
And the meadow's in   the   bloom,
234   (234) 345   345   (234) 234 345 (234) 234
While   the birds make music all the day.

Oh, When the Saints Go Marching In
234 345 (345) 456
Oh, when the saints
234 345 (345) 456
Go marching in,

234 345 (345) 456   345 234 345   (234)
Oh, when the saints go   marching in,
345 345 (234) 234   234 345 456 456   456 (45)
Oh Lord, I   want to   be   in   that   number
345 (345) 456   345 234 (234) 234
When the saints go   marching in!

The Streets of Laredo

456 456 (345) 345 (345) 456 (345) 345   (234) 234 (123)(12)
As   I   walked out in   the streets of   Laredo,
(12) 234 234   (234) 345 (345) 345 (234) 234 (234)
As   I   walked out in Laredo   one day,
456 456 (345) 345   (345) 456
I   spied a   young cowboy
(345) 345   (234) 234 (123)(12)
All wrapped in   white linen,
(12) 234   234 234   (234) 345
All wrapped in   white linen
(345) 345 (123)(123) 234
And cold as   the   clay.

Drink to Me Only with Thine Eyes

Here's a nice slow melody that gives us a good chance to
talk about hands. Up to now, all we have said about hold-
ing the harp is to hold it in your left hand between thumb
and forefinger. Now we are going to bring your right hand
into play. (If you are left-handed, you may want to re-
verse these directions.)

For slow songs you will often want to add some *vibrato*
on the sustained notes. (It goes over great around the
old campfire.) Let us explain what vibrato is by telling
you two possible ways to do it. You'll find the second
way especially useful in achieving blues effects.

Dan Smith

■ Hold the harmonica as below and bring the heels and fingertips of both hands together as if you were praying to a sideways god. By opening and closing this little "tent" while playing, you change the tone of the instrument.

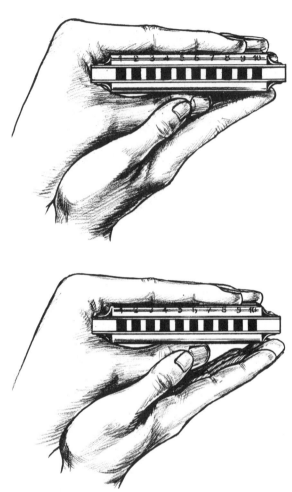

■ While keeping the heels of the hands together, bring the fingertips of the bottom hand around so that they curl slightly over the side of the top hand. The vibrato effect is achieved by uncurling and curling the fingers of the right hand.

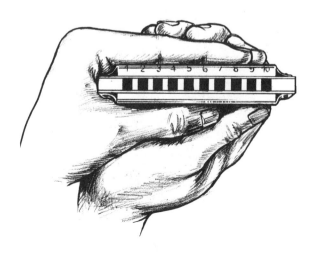

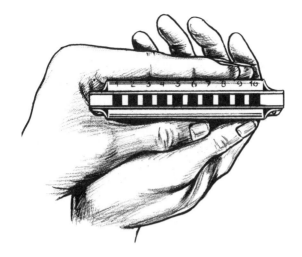

Try playing a few long chords and experimenting with different speeds of vibrato. When you have got it down, try using some on this tune: it's guaranteed to bring a tear to your eye.

Drink to Me Only with Thine Eyes
345   345   345 (345)(345)456(345) 345   (234)345
Drink to   me   only   with   thine   eyes
(345) 456 234(45) 345   (234)   234
And I   will pledge with   mine;
345 345   345 (345) (345)456 (345)345 (234)345
Or leave a   kiss   within   the   cup
(345) 456 234 (45) 345 (234) 234
And I'll   not ask for wine.
   456 456 345 456   567   456 456 345   456   456
   The thirst   that   from   the soul   doth rise
   456   (56) 456 456(345) 345 345(234)
   Doth ask a   drink   divine;
345 345   345 (345) (345)   456(345)345 (234)345
But might I   of   Jove's nectar   sip
(345) 456 234 (45) 345   (234) 234
I   would   not change for thine.

Single Notes

You have probably noticed that in most of our chord-melody songs there are one or two places where the chord is not exactly right. When you are playing solo, or even with someone providing a simple backup, most of these places are not too awful because they usually occur on unaccented notes of the melody. Sometimes all you need to do to clean up an awkward-sounding spot is to narrow down to a two-note chord instead of playing three notes. However, there are times when, even though you are playing the right melody note on top, none of the harmony notes below will sound quite right. This happens when the chord in the backup (or the chord you are hearing in your head) is neither I nor V. It can also happen if the melody note is a blow note and the back-up chord is a draw, or vice versa.

Now guitar players and piano players can play any chord they want under any given melody note, but what of the poor harp player? Are you doomed to forever play Stephen Foster melodies, cowboy ballads, and civil war songs? Of course not! We were just getting warmed up—now we are going to start to cook.

By now you ought to be pretty good at gauging the width of your "blowhole" to play either two notes or three at a time. Now it gets a little tougher: You are going to have to narrow down to blowing or drawing on only one hole. The principle is the same, but what makes it tricky is the increased need for accuracy. Follow this checklist as you try a nice, easy, single-note 4-blow:

- ■ keep the upper and lower lips fully relaxed
- ■ feel slight tension in the sides of the mouth (but not in the cheeks)
- ■ place the tongue on the "floor" of the mouth, keeping the throat open
- ■ breathe from the diaphragm

How does it sound? Okay? If you have any problems—now or ever—refer back to this checklist. Now play a single-note 4-draw. When you have a clear 4-blow and 4-draw, play this little melody on holes 345:

4 ④ 5 ④ 4 3 ③④ 4

You can play a major scale in single notes using the same pattern that you used for the chord-melody scales:

4 ④ 5 ⑤ 6 ⑥ ⑦ 7
Do re mi fa so la ti do

As a matter of fact, you can go over all of the tunes that we have done so far and play them in single-note style. Just use the highest number of each chord group.

Single-Note Tunes

Home, Sweet Home

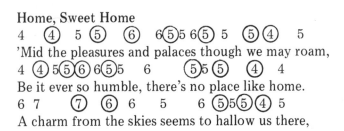

4   ④   5 ⑤   ⑥   6⑤5 6⑤ 5   ⑤④   5
'Mid the pleasures and palaces though we may roam,
4 ④5⑤⑥ 6⑤5   6   ⑤5⑤   ④   4
Be it ever so humble, there's no place like home.
6 7   ⑦   ⑥ 6   5   6 ⑤5⑤④ 5
A charm from the skies seems to hallow us there,

6   7   (7)   (6) 6   5 6   (5)5 (5) (4)   4
Which, seek through the world, is ne'er met with elsewhere.

Polly Wolly Doodle

"Polly Wolly Doodle" is a good tune for practicing tonguing. On the "polly wolly doodle" and "going to Louisiana" parts, you can *double-tongue*: Instead of repeating "too-too-too-too," whisper "too-koo-too-koo" into your harp.

Polly Wolly Doodle
4 (4) 5   5   4   4 (4) 5   5   4
Oh I went down South for to see my Sal,
   4   5 5 5 5   (5)(5)   5   5 (4)
   Sing polly wolly doodle all the day;
(3) (4)(4) (3)(3)(4) (4)(3)
My Sally am a spunky gal,
   (4)   6 6   6 6   (5)(5) (4)(4)   4
   Sing polly wolly doodle all the day.
4   (4)   5   4   (4)   5
Fare thee well, fare thee well,
4   (4)   5   5   (5)5 (4)
Fare thee well, my fairy fay,
(3) (3) (4)   (4)(4)(4)(3)(3)
For I'm going to Louisiana
(3) (3) (4) (4) (4)(4)(3)(3)
For to see my Susyanna,
   (4)   6 6   6 6   (5)(5) (4)(4)   4
   Sing polly wolly doodle all the day.

She'll Be Comin' round the Mountain

Be careful on this next one, as it goes up into the top octave (holes 7 through 10). In the top octave, the draw note of each hole is lower than the blow note—the opposite of the middle section (holes 4 through 6). Real quick—try this two-octave scale before you play the tune:

4	(4)	5	(5)	6	(6)	(7)	7	(8)	8	(9)	9	(10)	10
Do	re	mi	fa	so	la	ti	do	re	mi	fa	so	la	do

She'll Be Comin' round the Mountain
6   (6) 7 7 7   7 (6)   6   5   6 7
She'll be comin' round the mountain when she comes,
7   (8) 8 8 8   8   9   8   (8)   7 (8)
She'll be comin' round the mountain when she comes,
9   (9) 8 8 8   8 (8)   7
She'll be comin' round the mountain,
7   7 (6)(6) (6)   (6) (8)   7
She'll be comin' round the mountain,
(7) (6) 6 6 6   6   8 (8)   7   (7) 7
She'll be comin' round the mountain when she comes.

Tenting Tonight

"Tenting Tonight" is another tune in the upper register and also a good one for some tasteful vibrato. By the way, if you find that you are not getting enough air while playing, or if you tend to hyperventilate on certain tunes, try breathing through your nose when necessary. Opening up those sinuses also helps your tone.

Tenting Tonight

6   8 8 (8) 7   7 (7)(6) 7   6
We're tenting tonight on the old campground,
6 6 6 (5)   (5) 5
Give us a song to cheer
6 8 (8) 7   (7)(6) 7 6
Our weary hearts, a song of home
6 (7)   (7) (6)   6 7
And friends we love so dear.
  6 6 6 6   6   5 6 (6)(6) (6)(6)
Many are the hearts that are weary tonight,
  6 6 (6) (6) 7 7 (8)
Wishing for the war to cease;
8 8 8 (8) 7   7 (7)(6) (6) (6) 7 6
Many are the hearts that are looking for the right
7 8 7   8   (8) 7
To see the dawn of peace.
6   6   6 6   (6) (6) (6)(6)
Tenting tonight, tenting tonight,
6   6   6 6 (6) (7) 7
Tenting on the old campground.

The Camptown Races

6   6   5 6 (6) 6   5
Camptown ladies sing this song:
 345 (234) 345 (234)
 Doo - dah, doo-dah;
6   6   5 6 (6) 6   5
Camptown racetrack, five miles long,
(234)(345)345(234)234
 Oh, de doo-dah day.
4   4 5 6 7
Goin' to run all night,
(6) (6) 7 (6) 6
Goin' to run all day.
6 6 5 5   6 6 (6) 6   5
Bet my money on the bobtail nag;
(4)   5 (5) 5 (4) (4) 4
Somebody bet on the bay.

Notation

As we move along toward new and exciting harmonica horizons, we are going to need a more complete means of communicating musical ideas. The best way to do this is to give you the melodies in standard music notation along with the blow and draw hole numbers.

If you know how to read music, you will have no problem understanding the standard notation that follows, and you may want to skip ahead a bit.

The purpose of this section is not to teach you to read music, but rather to enable us to communicate better. In fact, reading music on the diatonic harmonica is not all that useful since every time you pick up a different key harp the notes are going to be in a different place. As a result few harp players are accomplished sight-readers (with the exception of chromatic players who play in all keys using a C harmonica).

Take your time with this material: just being able to read a little of the notation will help you get the feeling for the rhythm of a riff or phrase more easily. In addition, if you play another instrument, you will be able to sound out each example before attempting it on the harmonica.

Rhythm

The most important aspects that any notation system can convey are *melody* and *rhythm*. Until this point, we have used blow and draw hole numbers to indicate the melody, but we have not been able to notate the rhythm. Standard notation will allow us to do this. Let's look at a few examples.

In the example above, there are three kinds of notes: the *quarter note*, the *half note*, and the *whole note*.

quarter note: ♩

half note: ♩

whole note: o

The *time signature* ($\frac{4}{4}$) at the beginning tells you that this music is in "four-four" time. This means that there are four *beats* to each *measure* and that a quarter note receives one beat. A half note receives two beats and the whole note takes up a whole measure of four beats.

Now try playing these four measures. Tap your foot in a steady rhythm as you count 1 2 3 4 to yourself.

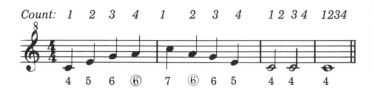

To begin playing the music that follows, you also need to know about eighth notes, triplets, rests, and ties.

Eighth notes are played twice as fast as quarter notes. Try playing the example below counting 1 & 2 & 3 & 4 &. Tap your foot in quarter-note rhythm. Play one eighth-note as you tap and the next eighth note when your foot comes up.

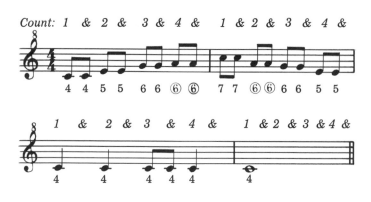

Triplets are played three to the beat. Play this example carefully, making sure that all the notes are evenly spaced and that the beat remains steady.

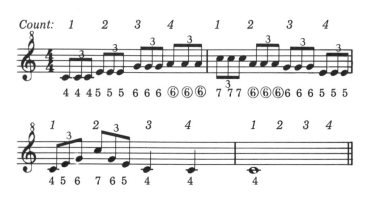

Rests indicate silence. Each note value has a corresponding rest:

whole note	o	—	whole rest
half note	𝅗𝅥	▬	half rest
quarter note	♩	𝄽	quarter rest
eighth note	♪	𝄾	eighth rest

Now here's a swinging version of our four-measure riff which includes rests.

We use a *tie* to tie two notes together like this:

The first note is played and held through the value of the note to which it is tied. Before playing this next variation, try counting out loud and clapping the rhythm.

To finish up this section, here's a boogie-woogie progression that uses everything that we have just gone over. You are on your own with the counting. The back-up chords above the music will work if you are playing a C harp.

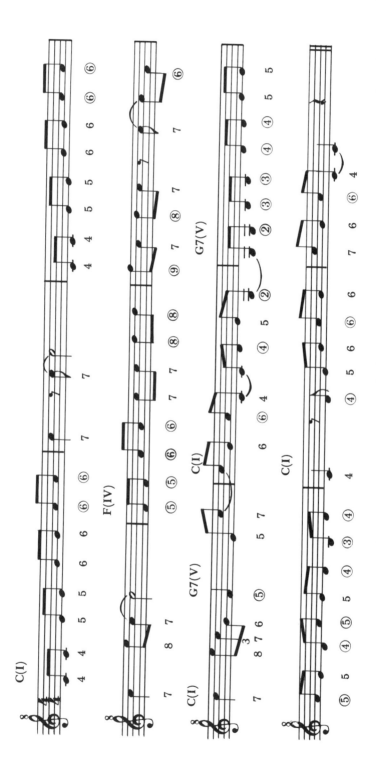

THE BLUES

The boogie-woogie solo you played in the last section begins to sound pretty hip, doesn't it? But wait—there's more. Everything that we have played so far has been what harmonica players call *straight-harp* playing. This means that we have been playing in the key stamped on the harp. What we are going to do now is to play in a different key. The simplest and most common way of playing harmonica in the "wrong" key is called *cross harp*.

In cross-harp playing you get the I chord by *drawing*, instead of *blowing* as in straight harp. The easiest way to begin to understand cross harp is to start right in playing.

Take a look at this riff that was part of the boogie-woogie solo in the last section.

What we are going to do is to make this the beginning of a new solo. It is the same chord progression but in a new key (G, if you have a C harp).

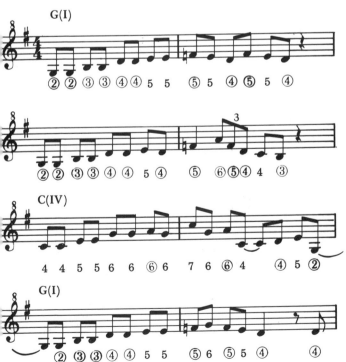

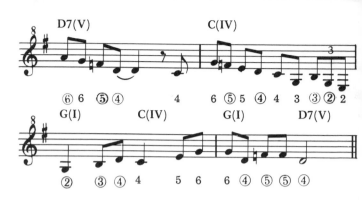

Here are some simple cross-harp riffs to help you get the idea. We will use a new musical symbol here called the *slur*. A slur looks just like a tie except that it joins two or more different notes.

When you see notes joined by a slur, play them in one breath by sliding the harp (as opposed to tonguing each note individually).

These riffs all end on the cross-harp I chord. The basic twelve-bar blues progression has I, IV, and V chords arranged like this:

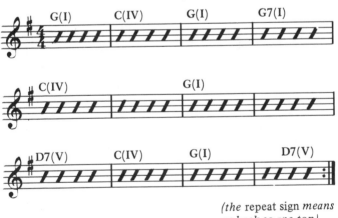

(the repeat sign *means go back to the top)*

Since the blow chord is your IV chord in cross-harp playing, you know that any blow note will work on the IV. On the V chord you need to be more careful. The best thing to do is to use a riff, similar to those above, that leads very definitely back to I.

Here are two complete twelve-bar blues solos to get you off and running. Try to get some musical friend to back you up while you play them. When you have mastered these you will have a pretty good idea of how to find your way around in cross harp.

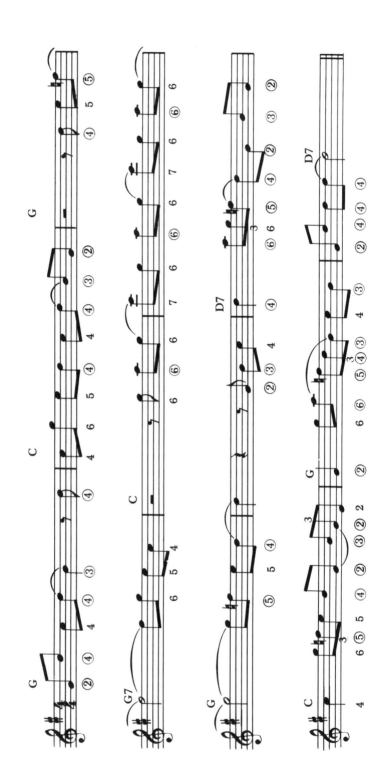

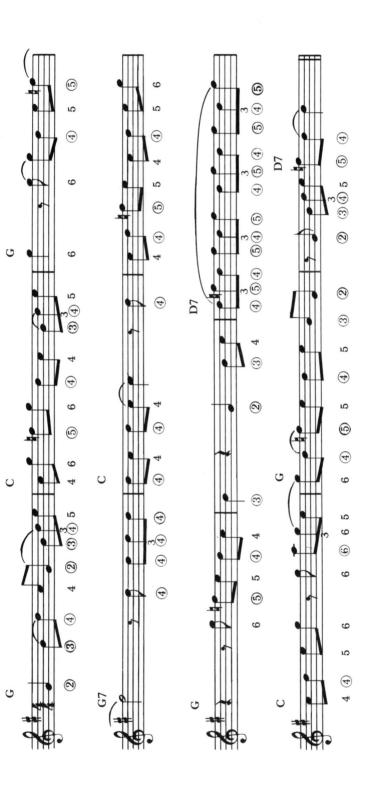

Bending Notes

When the harmonica was invented it was most assuredly not meant to play the blues. Its fixed reeds were more suited to playing polkas, marches, dance tunes, and other melodies that did not depend upon the many flatted notes which are the mainstay of the blues. It was a particular brand of genius that discovered that the little, rigid reeds could be made to bend and twist and give up notes, growls, and whispers that they did not even know they had.

It is very difficult to teach someone to bend a note: So much of the technique depends on your experiencing the feeling of actually doing it. In the final analysis you will have to keep trying the suggestions given here until a moment comes when your ears, mouth, tongue, and mind all unite and exclaim, "Hey, we've got it!"

Below are a series of descriptions designed to put you in the mood for bending notes. Some are technical, for the science-minded among you. Some are more or less physical description of how your tongue, mouth, and diaphragm react, for the would-be doctors out there. The rest are analogies that we thought up late at night after all else had failed. (These last are probably the ones that will work!)

■ Technically speaking, bending a note has to do with distorting the way that a reed vibrates in the air stream. Normally the reed vibrates freely as the air passes over its most flexible part, the tip. When you narrow the air stream, by puckering determinedly and dropping your jaw slightly (which increases the cavity of your mouth), you also direct the air over the thicker part of the reed. This thicker part vibrates more slowly and therefore sounds a lower pitch.

■ Pretend that you are about to give someone a rather large, intense kiss. When we actually do kiss someone (on the cheek, for example) we do not involve our throat or diaphragm. Instead we just suck a little air into our mouth. Now picture kissing a porous surface: In order to keep kissing, you need to draw the air down into your throat and then into your chest, using your diaphragm to create the vacuum that draws the air in.

■ Whistle a midrange note while breathing in. Now let the note slide down to the lowest note that you can whistle. Notice how your mouth changes: the tongue comes up in back, down in front; the throat opens up and the jaw drops.

■ Pretend that you are drinking through a straw but

that the straw goes directly to the bottom of your stomach: Suck the air in from all the way down there.

■ Think the note lower. After all is said and done, this is probably the most powerful suggestion. If you can visualize it (or, more correctly, "hear" it in your mind's ear), your body is going to figure out a way of actually accomplishing it. You can be sure that the first person to bend a note was no physics professor. . . .

The important thing is to practice every day and to listen to master players bending notes on recordings. Don't get discouraged. Until everything falls into place, it is going to be difficult, but it gets easier all the time. In no time—if you practice hard— you might become rather bent yourself!

We suggest that you start with the ④ and ⑤ draw holes, which, in our opinion, are the easiest to bend at first. Actually, the matter of which notes are easiest to bend for you depends on several factors, among them: the type and key of harmonica you are using, how well the harp is broken in, and the actual size and shape of your mouth. Keep trying until you find one note that you can bend easily and consistently. Then try the others.

Here is a chart of which notes can be bent by overdrawing and overblowing.

hole	1	2	3	4	5	6	7	8	9	10
blow bends							B	D E^b	F $F\sharp$	B^b B
blow	C	E	G	C	E	G	C	E	G	C
draw	D	G	B	D	F	A	B	D	F	A
draw bends	D^b	F$\sharp$ F	B^b A A^b	D^b C	E	A^b				
hole	1	2	3	4	5	6	7	8	9	10

John Mayall and Albert King

Riffs

The riffs that follow are similar to the last batch except that they incorporate bent notes. We will use this symbol to indicate a note that is bent:

On holes 2, 3, 4, 8, 9, and 10 there are more than one bent note available. To indicate how far to bend, we will put slash marks through the arrow—one for each additional bend below the first—like this:

Don't worry if you cannot get every note clearly in the example above. These double bends—especially on ③ — require a bit of experience. In addition, your instrument must be broken in well. The more you practice bending accurately to the note you want, the more experience you get and the more broken in the reed becomes.

Below are basic riffs that you can then use in any way you like. Take time to fool around with these riffs— change the rhythm, the tonguing and slurring, string several of them together, etc. If any particular one gives you trouble—say, with a difficult bend or a tricky rhythm— try to change it around to get a similar musical idea that is comfortable for you to play. In this way you will be laying the foundation of your personal style. Any riff that really strikes your fancy—it could be just two or three notes in a particular order and rhythm—should be practiced over and over until it becomes part of you. All players have a handful of these that are like old friends that they can call on whenever need be. If they are distinctive and original enough, they become trademarks of the player's style.

Junior Wells

Soloing on the Blues

To play a blues solo, all you have to do is string a bunch of riffs together. To play a *good* blues solo, you have to do more. Start with one idea—it can be really simple—and build on it. Everything that follows must develop logically from what has come before. Learn the following solos note for note: They have been carefully thought out to point you in the right direction. Create your own solos based on your own ideas and learn them just as studiously.

Once you have learned to walk, you can begin to run. Start improvising and let the inspiration of the moment carry you along. Keep listening to what you are playing with an objective ear and keep asking yourself if your playing makes sense. If your musical message is not clear to you, it cannot be clear to anyone else.

Keeping all this in mind, remember also that creativity cannot grow in a vacuum. If you are not already listening to recordings of the greats, now is the time to start. If you are not sure just where to start, check the discography in this book. When you hear a harp riff or solo that you really like, take time to analyze it and find out why it moves you. Copying riffs and entire solos can be a painless and extremely helpful learning experience. Even if you never use a particular note-for-note riff that you have "copped" in this manner, the practice and understanding gained will subtly enrich your playing. It is sort of like the staid classical guitarist who was heard to remark, after hearing a recording of one of Jimi Hendrix's more outlandish solos, "I wish that I were able to do that—and then I never would."

As you get into the following solo, you will notice that the basic idea is summed up in this one snazzy riff that kicks it off:

Try to identify the different parts of the riff as it comes back in bits and pieces. Notice how the same bunch of notes may be placed over the I, IV, or V chord. There may be dissonance in places, but that is part of what the blues is about.

The following solo is of a more progressive nature. Although it works tolerably well against a standard twelve-bar blues progression, make an effort to hear the jazzier chord changes as written. There are two new techniques in this one: overblowing and hitting a bent note head-on (without bending down to it from the natural note).

The feeling of overblowing is somewhat different from that of overdrawing. Although you must still think the note lower, your tongue and mouth behave differently. Since the blow reed is on the bottom reed plate, you must do what amounts to the opposite of what you do to bend a draw note: You must constrict the cavity of your mouth by bringing the tongue up in the middle. To go back to one of our analogies for note-bending: whistle a midrange note and then let it slide up to the highest note you can whistle. Note the action of the tongue, and make sure that the mouth keeps relaxed.

To jump directly to a bent note, you have to be fairly sure of yourself. Play a bend that is easy for you; bend it down from the natural note a few times until you really have the feel of it down. Now try hitting it head-on. If you have trouble, try "popping" into the bent note with the back of your throat. This is sort of like swallowing but more like saying the letter K while breathing in. The sudden rush of air pressure can help you to hit the note you want. Throat popping can also be a gutsy style of tonguing (especially useful on the low notes).

Muddy Waters and Jerry Portnoy

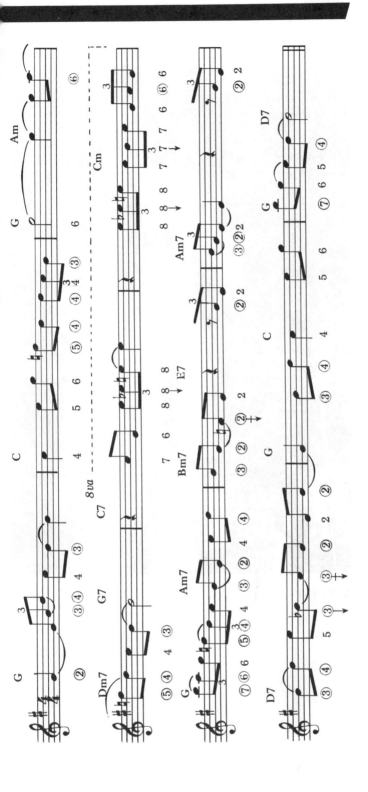

That's about it for soloing on the blues. If you can play all the stuff in this chapter, you can play anything. Plus you have all of those ideas of your own that you have come up with, right?

Little Walter

HARMONICA STYLES

There are as many harp styles as there are harp players. Although there exist broad, general categories—folk, blues, rock, jazz—many factors go into determining or defining a style. City players, country players, black players, white players, all come into contact with different music and life experiences, all of which go into forming their styles. Another factor is purely physical: There are certain techniques that are used in one style that are simply not used in others. For instance, *tongue-blocking* is used by many country players to create a light, clean, many-noted style by facilitating skips from one note to another. On the other hand, lip puckering, the single-note technique we have been using throughout this book, lends itself to an emotional, hot style with lots of overtones, ghosted notes, and raw power—just the thing for Chicago-style blues. Then you have the great country blues player Sonny Terry, who uses a combination of tongue-blocking, lip-puckering, throat pops, as well as vocal whoops and hollers to get his unique sound.

The following are some personal observations and advice as to what makes one style sound different from another. For everything we say, you might find an example that breaks the rule but, after all, that is what good music is really all about: breaking new ground.

Folk Harmonica

Generally speaking, folk harmonica is straight harp. The tunes that we played at the beginning of this book are good examples of the folk style. A harmonica played this way should sound like something that would not be out of place around a cozy campfire; it should remind you of the end of an episode of *The Waltons* ("...Good-night John Boy...678"). This is not to say that folk harp is necessarily sentimental or wimpy. It can also have the powerful honesty that players like Bob Dylan and Woody Guthrie brought to it. Listen to Woody's "Goin' down This Long, Dusty Road" or "(If You Ain't Got the) Dough-Re-Mi" and Dylan's "Blowin' in the Wind" or "Just Like a Woman."

Levon Helm and Bob Dylan

Folk harp can be an exacting, single-note style or a completely chordal accompaniment wash or a combination of the two. The one thing you hardly ever do in the folk style is to bend notes.

Blues Harmonica

Blues harp is not one style but many. It is probably the style with the single greatest number of master practitioners past and present—not to mention the most amateurs. Players like Sonny Terry, Little Walter, Sonny Boy Williamson, Rice Miller, Big Walter Horton, Junior Wells, James Cotton, Four City Joe, and Paul Butterfield would probably all consider themselves blues-harp players although their styles and techniques differ considerably. Sonny Boy Williamson spent most of his life in rural Arkansas and developed a country blues style that employed a lot of bending, and numerous vocal and hand effects. James Cotton—one of the string of master players who got their start in the late, great Muddy Waters's band—started out a country boy, copying the style of Sonny Boy Williamson. Upon Cotton's arrival in Chicago, he found that people in the blues scene there did not approve of his down-home style. It took him years to relearn the instrument and begin playing the highly rhythmic, swinging, Chicago-style harp that his predecessor in Muddy's band, Little Walter, had made famous.

Chicago blues, and blues harp in general, favors the cross-harp position (sometimes called *second position*, straight harp being *first position*). In cross harp you play a lot of bends but you play them in two ways: You slur down from the natural note to the bent one *or* you go directly to the bent note, a task that takes a lot of practice. We talked a bit about this in the "Soloing on the Blues" chapter. Here is an exercise to help you get it down. It is based on one developed by Charlie McCoy, a country-style master who loves the blues.

Charlie McCoy, Jason Shulman, and James Cotton in Nashville

Although hitting a bent note like this is not actually a special effect per se, this may be a good time to talk about some other devices which may be considered a bit more flamboyant. The first is the *head-shake* or *head vibrato.* All you do is move your head (and therefore your mouth) back and forth very rapidly between two notes. Try it with ④ and ⑤ , and you'll get the idea.

While we are talking about single-note playing, you should know that there are a number of other positions besides straight harp (first) and cross harp (second) that are available to you if your single-note technique is clean. Junior Wells often plays in fourth position, using the 2-blow as the tonic. This gives you a minor scale (technically called the Phrygian mode) that can get real low-down mournful. Here is a complete fourth-position scale:

Try these brief examples. If you have a C harp, you will be playing in E minor.

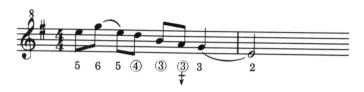

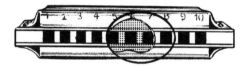

You can hear that the second note of the scale is a little funky sounding. You will want to avoid it most of the time, but it can be really effective when used deliberately against the V chord.

Tongue-blocking is a method of getting single notes that gives you greater alacrity in skipping around the harp than the pucker method we have been using. What you do is cover four holes of the harp with your mouth opening but then block out three of them with the tongue.

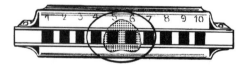

Try placing your mouth and tongue as in the picture above. When you are comfortable and are getting a clear blow 8, shift your tongue over to the left so that you are playing a blow 5. It feels pretty awkward at first—some people never get used to it—but it comes in handy on fast runs that skip notes of the scale. Tongue-blocking can also help in bending notes if you block part of the hole you are bending.

There are a few special effects that employ tongue-blocking. You can play your melody note on top and then provide a rhythmic chordal accompaniment below by unblocking and blocking the adjacent holes. You can play in octaves by using the *underside* of the tongue to block the holes, leaving one hole unblocked on either side of the tongue.

Another effect, which is used often in blues playing is the *octave tremolo*. This is achieved by alternating between the note to the right and the note to the left of the tongue. To keep it under control, it is best to actually move the tongue as little as possible but rather roll it back and forth.

The effects described above are not limited to blues playing. In fact, tongue-blocking to play single notes is used extensively by country players; the octave style shows up in many rock rhythm-fills; and the rhythmic chordal accompaniment idea is basically a folk-style device.

Jazz and Pop Harmonica

There are two major names here: Toots Thielemans and Stevie Wonder. Toots is the apotheosis of jazz harp. He plays chromatic harmonica exclusively, making extensive use of the keys of F-sharp, A-flat, E-flat, and F. Stevie plays mostly chromatic, but has been known to employ a diatonic harp now and then. As far as jazz is concerned, the only real way to do it is on the chromatic.

In case you have never seen a chromatic harmonica up close, here is a diagram showing the notes available. (This is the layout of the popular Hohner *Chromonica 260*.)

	hole	1	2	3	4	5	6	7	8	9	10
slide out	blow	C	E	G	C	C	E	G	C	C	E
	draw	D	F	A	B	D	F	A	B	D	F
slide in	blow	C#	E#	G#	C#	C#	E#	G#	C#	C#	E#
	draw	D#	F#	A#	B#	D#	F#	A#	B#	D#	F#

You can see right away that this is a very different animal from our old pal, the diatonic. The only similarity occurs on holes 5 through 8, which correspond to holes 4 through 7 on the diatonic. The slide makes it like having two harmonicas: Leave it out and you have a C harp, push it in and you have a C-sharp harp. Each position gives you two notes (blow and draw) per hole, making a total of four notes available just standing still. To make it even more confusing, some of the notes repeat on the same hole. For instance, look at hole number 2. Slide out gives you E and F; slide in gives you E-sharp and F-sharp. Since there is only a half step between E and F, E-sharp sounds the same as F. (They are what we call *enharmonic* equivalents.)

Don't let all this technical talk scare you away from chromatic harp forever. Try to get your hands on one and just fool around for awhile. It will start to make sense quickly.

The great blues harpist Junior Wells makes interesting use of the chromatic's low bass notes by playing a C instrument in D minor (third position—see below). In this position you do not have to use the slide and it is rather easy to get a mellow, minor, very bluesy sound.

Toots Thielemans

There are ways to get a jazz sound out of the diatonic harmonica. The easiest way is to play in *third position*. Third position uses ④ as its tonic. This is another minor sounding position (technically called the Dorian mode). Here is a third-position scale and two characteristic riffs:

And here is a third-position jazz tune (C harp plays in D minor):

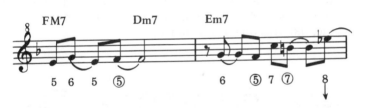

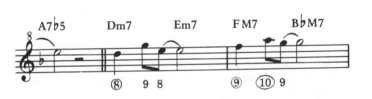

Country Harmonica

When you talk about country-style harp, you have got to talk about Charlie McCoy. Charlie started out wanting to play exactly like Little Walter but, lucky for us, he developed his own unique style. Although his style is influenced by his Nashville location (where he plays on just about every recording session that uses harp), he has played nearly every kind of music there is, backing up artists as diverse as Roy Orbison, Perry Como, Simon and Garfunkel, and Elvis Presley. If you ever come across any of Charlie's solo albums on the Monument label, snap them up whatever the cost.

A lot of country harp playing can be characterized as coming from the "straight-harp/high-end" school. This differs dramatically from most blues playing in which you hang out down around ②, ③, and ④. The reason that country players stay above the 4 hole is that this enables them to get a pure, unadulterated major scale, which is the basis of most country-style music. Try figuring out some simple fiddle tunes like "Turkey in the Straw" or "Soldier's Joy" to see what we mean. You can get a lot of pretty little scale runs right around the 7 hole, like this one, for instance:

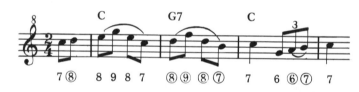

Also, remember all of the bends possible on holes 7, 8, 9, and 10. If you can stand the shrillness, you can get some really hip Mickey Mouse blues.

Of course, a lot of country playing is done in cross harp as well. In addition, many country-western players use somewhat exotic instruments to add different colorings. Mickey Raphael, who plays with Willie Nelson, makes extensive use of a bass harmonica. Playing very simple

Neil Young

lines made up of sustained tones, he gives the effect of an expressive accordion. Hohner's *Echo Harp* is also sometimes heard in the background of the Nashville Sound.

Rock Harmonica

As far as the harmonica is concerned, rock is simply an extension of the blues. That is, any blues riff could work with just about any rock song. It really comes down to a matter of taste and what you consider rock. Harp can be heard on recordings by The Beatles, The Rolling Stones, The J. Geils Band, Bruce Springsteen, Bonnie Raitt, and so on, and so on. All of them play rock, but each of them plays different.

One thing that you might notice when you hear good rock players is that they are not coming (à la Dylan) from a folk bag. They tend to think of their harps as horns. They play simple but very effective "horn lines" on their powerfully amplified instruments. You will find it easy to pick out these rudimentary punctuations just by listening carefully to what the horn sections are doing on your favorite records.

For some rock styles, your standard blues riffs may be a bit too intense. Rock is for the most part major in tonality, while blues walks the line between major and minor. In fact, a lot of rock is played straight-harp.

One thing that goes for any kind of rock music is that it is generally played LOUDER than any other kind of music. If you are going to play in a rock band, you are going to need some help to be heard. Here are a few tips about the kind of sound equipment you will need.

Amplified Harmonica

The first link in the chain is the *microphone*. Some players get very particular about the type of mic that they use. This is understandable, since the quality of the mic can make or break a great sound. Beyond quality, the most important aspect of the microphone is how easy it is to hold. There is a knack to cupping the mic securely in your hands and still being able to hold on to the harp. To make it easy, you need a mic that is small and light.

As to specifics, you will want your mic to be *unidirectional* (cuts down on feedback), *dynamic* or *ribbon* type (doesn't distort when you jam your harp right up to it), and either *high impedance* (to go into an instrument amplifier) or *low impedance* (to go directly into a mixing board).

There is no specific mic technique that works with every mic. Just remember that the overall sound and tone color of your playing is determined by the resonant cavity of your mouth. Any mic will respond best to this if you keep it positioned directly opposite your mouth as much as possible.

You will want a long mic *cord* to give you freedom to move around. A good, heavy-duty cord may seem expensive, but it is worth it. A cheap cord that shorts out after being stepped on a couple of times, or one that develops an annoying snap-crackle-pop in one of the plugs the third time you used it, is not worth a dime. It is also a very good idea to have a spare cord on hand. Coiled cords are nice because they cannot get tangled. However, if you jump around a lot, the springlike recoil can get to be a drag or, worse yet, could yank the mic out of your hands.

Now you have a mic and a cord, but you need a place to plug in. If you have a good sound system and someone trustworthy to run it, you may want to plug directly

Paul Butterfield and Rick Danko

into the board. This means that you relinquish control of tone and reverb settings. It also means that the only way you can hear yourself is through the monitor speakers.

For most situations, your best bet is to have your own *amplifier*. This way, you can set (and reset) the tone and reverb controls the way you like them. You do not need anything really powerful: A small amp of 60 or 80 watts is adequate for most club situations; if you play larger halls, you should be putting all of the instruments through the PA anyway. Even if your amp is miked or fed into the mixing board through a direct box, having the amp on stage helps you (and the other musicians) hear what you are playing and how you sound.

A FINAL NOTE

If you've gotten through the book and have arrived here at the end, our congratulations! You have come from an initial interest, and perhaps love, of the instrument to actually being able to play it in a number of different styles. You have learned a little about its history and the players who have unlocked its secrets. You know how to play in different positions and keys and have an idea of the way your harp should sound when you are using it to play folk tunes, blues, jazz and rock.

Soon you may start making your own unique contributions—find a new position, invent a new effect, figure out a run that no one thought could be played. Or maybe your association with the harmonica will remain private: You will keep it in your pocket and only pull it out to play when you are alone. . . .

Whatever you do from this point on is up to you. You have arrived at a stage where you can begin to learn easily from other players, records, and books. Remember: Have fun and do your best to give pleasure to others— that's what playing the harmonica (and music in general) is all about.

Paul Oscher, harmonica player with Muddy Waters's 1969 band

POSITION CHART

With the aid of this chart you can tell at a glance what key harmonica you will need to play in second, third, or fourth position in any key.

Since some keys can have two names, we have included a table of enharmonic equivalents. If you want to play in a key that is not listed in the first column of the transposition chart, find it in the bottom row of the enharmonic equivalents and note its other name directly above.

key you want to play in	harp key		
	cross harp (second position)	third position	fourth position
A	D	G	F
B♭	E♭	A♭	F♯
B	E	A	G
C	F	B♭	A♭
D♭	F♯	B	A
D	G	C	B♭
E♭	A♭	D♭	B
E	A	D	C
F	B♭	E♭	D♭
F♯	B	E	D
G	C	F	E♭
A♭	D♭	F♯	E

Enharmonic Equivalents

B♭	B	C	D♭	E♭	E	F	F♯	A♭
A♯	C♭	B♯	C♯	D♯	F♭	E♯	G♭	G♯

BIBLIOGRAPHY

Gindick, John. *The Natural Blues and Country Western Harmonica: A Beginner's Guide.* San Diego: The Cross Harp Press, 1977.

Gindick, John. *Rock 'n' Blues Harmonica.* San Diego: The Cross Harp Press. 1982.

Glover, Tony "Harp Dog." *Blues Harp Songbook.* New York: Oak Publications, 1975.

Glover, Tony "Little Sun." *Blues Harp.* New York: Oak Publications, 1965.

Glover, Tony. *Rock Harp.* New York: Oak Publications, 1981.

Hunter, Richard. *Jazz Harp.* New York: Oak Publications, 1980.

Terry, Sonny; Cooper, Kent; and Palmer, Fred. *The Harp Styles of Sonny Terry.* New York: Oak Publications, 1975.

DISCOGRAPHY

Blues

Sonny Terry
Sonny Terry: Harmonica and Vocal Solos   Folkways FA 2035
Midnight Special   Fantasy F-24721

Sonny Boy Williamson (I)
Sonny Boy Williamson   Blues Classics 3

Sonny Boy Williamson (II)
Sonny Boy Williamson (II): This Is My   Chess 2CH 50027
  Story
The Original Sonny Boy Williamson (II)   Blues Classics 9

Little Walter
Little Walter: Boss Blues Harmonica   Chess 2CH 60014
Muddy Waters (Blues Masters Vol. III)   Chess 2ACMB-203

Little Walter/Walter Horton
McKinley Morgenfield a.k.a. Muddy   Chess 2CH 60006
  Waters

James Cotton
Taking Care of Business   Capitol ST 814

Country

Charlie McCoy
The Real McCoy   Monument 231329
The World of Charlie McCoy   Monument 18097

Norton Buffalo
Desert Horizon   Capitol SW-11847

Mickey Raphael
Willie and Family—Live   Columbia 35642

Rock

Stevie Wonder
Fulfillingness First Finale   Tamala T6 33251

Paul Butterfield
Levon Helm and the RCO Allstars   ABC AA-1017

Bruce Springsteen
Darkness on the Edge of Town   Columbia JC 35318

Jazz

Toots Thielemans
Captured Live   Choice CRS1007

Folk

Bob Dylan
Blonde on Blonde   Columbia C2S 841
Greatest Hits   Columbia KCS 9463